T0375602

HOW
THE LOVE OF GOD
— RESCUED ME FROM ABUSE —

FROM

FEAR TO FAITH

MY LIFE WITH GOD

ROSALIND STEWART

WestBow Press books may be ordered through booksellers or by contacting:

WestBow Press
A Division of Thomas Nelson & Zondervan
1663 Liberty Drive
Bloomington, IN 47403
www.westbowpress.com
844-714-3454

ISBN: 979-8-3850-2672-2 (sc)
ISBN: 979-8-3850-2673-9 (hc)
ISBN: 979-8-3850-2674-6 (e)

Library of Congress Control Number: 2024911064

Print information available on the last page.

WestBow Press rev. date: 6/28/2024

Contents

Restoring Your Territory and Freedom

Growing in Faith and Hope

Foreword

The truth is I have really struggled with writing this book because I need to share enough of my past with you to help you understand the change that has taken place. This means returning to a place I do not want to be because it had so much pain, hurt, heartache, and non-stop tears. My sister once heard me crying while I was asleep and had to ask me in the morning what was wrong. So when I say non-stop tears, I mean it, and not because I was a prima donna princess who was not getting her way because I was in a perpetual pit of despair with no foreseeable way of getting out.

The image I held of my life was of me drowning in an ocean with waves crashing all over me. While trying desperately to swim to the top of the ocean to gasp for air, another wave would come crashing down on top of me, pulling me under again. I felt utterly exhausted and was barely staying alive emotionally.

This is why I love God so much. He literally saved me from drowning to death. I am no longer destroyed or nearly killed by my circumstances, because in the middle of the storms of life, I have learnt that God alone is my stability. He is my rock—my safe place to land.

So, no matter how much I may get tossed about, all I have to do is to keep holding on to God. Then nothing can destroy me emotionally.

But this change is a journey. You don't begin anchored in faith. Usually you are drifting along, being tossed about by your circumstances, until you get so sick and tired of life and desperate enough that you will try anything.

That's when God can become the anchor point in your life. Your external situation will not change automatically, but internally, you will begin to find a stability that gives you hope, peace, joy, and strength in life's storms, giving you the ability to keep fighting on and to make the changes you need to with God at your side.

If this sounds wishy-washy, it's not. I will give you personal examples of what God has taught me and how he comes through time and time again in practical ways, teaching me that he is there in every circumstance, no matter how big or small, as long as I depend on him and not myself.

Like the time when I wanted lemons but they were too expensive for me to buy. The next day, a woman got on the bus with me and randomly offered everyone on the bus lemons because her tree had produced too many.

The time I secretly wanted to have my very own bottle of perfume, yet I couldn't even afford to buy spray deodorant from the supermarket. Then, my Dad's cousin came for a visit from Ireland. I had barely got to see her during her brief stay because I was working. But when I returned home the evening she left, I found a whole bottle of proper perfume waiting for me on my pillow. I never mentioned it and she had no idea that it was a secret petition of my heart and I hadn't even prayed about it.

The time I had to get a dining table and chairs but couldn't afford it, so I went to the local St Vincent de Paul shop and got a set for $130, which I later found out had cost between $600 and $700 in the shop. But what got me was that the week before, I had missed out on another dining set because I was worried about spending a whole $110. So I didn't buy it and when I went back the next week, it was sold. But the difference was it was an old 70s-style dining set with unattractive bright green textured material. The actual table God had reserved for me was modern and the exact colour of the rest of my lounge furniture I had at home, so it suited perfectly.

The time I went to a U2 concert and got front row three nights running. On the third night, I made a pact with the man I was standing beside in the line that we would save a spot for each other. I just got there first and held his spot.

Then years later, I went to another U2 concert and had no one to go with. As I got into the stadium, I saw at the front row a one-person spot, which I ran for and got. It was right at the front row so I screamed with exhilaration—more accurately, I gave out an almighty shrill.

I turned to the people on either side of me and apologised for my scream and as I turned to the second person, he smiled and I smiled back. It was the very man, now with his son, that I had sat with all those years ago at the other concert, so I wasn't alone.

And the time I really wanted a particular U2 song, which was a duet. A week or so later, what randomly comes in the mail but two copies of a CD with all of U2's duets, including the very song I wanted and, again, I hadn't even prayed for it.

> Delight yourself in the Lord, and he will give you the desires of your heart. (Psalm 37:4 ESV)

You see, you can't tell me God doesn't exist. I've had too many experiences that prove he does. But that's the fun part and that's another book, which I'll share with you later.

Introduction

> There is no fear in love, but perfect love casts out fear. (1 John 4:18 ESV)

When you know that God loves you, it removes all the power that fear holds over your life. But how does this happen?

It happens when you experience God's love for you through his provision and protection. Then his love for you and your faith in him becomes your focus and your reality. It becomes your dependency, what you lean on, rely on, and have confidence in, and not the fear in your life.

You can then give God full control over your life and not the fear. As you learn you no longer have to fight the fear on your own but that you have God on your side, this is how fear loses it power over you.

> For I, the Lord your God, hold your right hand;
> it is I who say to you, 'Fear not, I am the one who helps you'. (Isaiah 41:13 ESV)

Fear is simply a tool the devil uses to control, trap, and paralyse you and he will use it in a myriad of ways: through our minds, our circumstances, and other people.

The Bible describes the devil's purpose as this: 'The thief comes only to steal and kill and destroy'. But Jesus came to counter this, saying, "I came that they may have life and have it abundantly. I am the good shepherd. The good shepherd lays down his life for the sheep". (John10:10–11 ESV)

I am writing this as a book of praise to God for all he has done for me by telling the world how much I love God and why. God is simply over and beyond anything that I could ever dare to dream or imagine.

God was there for me when I felt no one else was, and he loved me when I felt no one else did. God alone brought me from fear to faith and this book is about my life with God. But first, I have to tell you a bit about my life when it was without God.

Fear Takes Hold

CHAPTER 1

Ireland

I REMEMBER PARTS OF MY TEN AND A HALF YEARS GROWING UP in Ireland, before my family and I moved to Australia. Things like making mud pies with my siblings and playing games outside, which was where we seemed to always be, then playing with Barbies, dressing up, and watching TV.

We played games with our next door neighbour. Like the time we were in their kitchen and everyone was standing in a circle, singing and dancing to the song 'Hokey Pokey'.

When I was very young, I apparently woke up one snowy winter's night, and repeatedly went into my parents' bed only to be lifted back into my own. So I left my house, and I walked to my neighbours, apparently hopping right in between the parents who were in their bed.

I was discovered after my dad felt a chilly breeze and went to investigate, only to find the front door wide open and little footsteps in the snow, which he followed right to our neighbours' house.

He found me snuggled in between our neighbours, fast asleep. Dad left me there to sleep, as he was told to leave me be and they'd bring me home in the morning.

When I had returned to Ireland for the first time since immigrating, I went to visit their house and as soon the front door was opened, I burst into tears. I had no idea I felt like this or that my grief was still so strong over ten years on.

There were other families we were very close too who we would go to swimming, speech and drama, Girl Guides, and school with. I remember playing dress up at their houses, going on adventure walks, and doing homework.

One of the families had a farm, so we would put on our welly boots, grab an apple from their orchard, and go to see their cows and pigs, then look at the horses in the field as we walked to a little shop to get some sweets. That's the essence of how I see myself: in welly boots playing in the mud, exploring outside with the animals, and just happily having fun.

One of these families were my godparents and their children, who I loved dearly, and again with them, it was dress ups, playing, and just being kids. I remember when their dog had puppies, these big, pudgy pups which I loved and got to play with.

Anyway, with my relatives it was exactly the same: all great memories. My cousin and I were best friends. Playing with our siblings, we pretended we were school teachers ticking each others' make believe answers, taking turns to be the teacher and students. Then we'd all pretend to be shipwrecked on an adventure island and we had to get home safely before we got captured by the baddies. We had so much fun, always playing, even on the tractor in their neighbours' yard.

Then at Coney Island, where my granny and relatives lived, we'd play at the seaside and walk around the island with my dad and go into to the village, which was a proper fishing port where the pungent smell of fish and the sea was actually nice.

As a family, we would go to Gortin Glen going for walks in the forest, which was beautiful and so much fun to explore and Port Salon for holidays.

At home I remember Mum making lunches in neatly packed boxes with biscuits for snacks; pulling down our cuffs from under our jumpers; making sure we were neat and tidy before school; and blow drying our hair. Being our constant chauffeur, driving us to and from speech and drama, ballet, horse riding, gymnastics, swimming, and Girl Guides.

Dad would read us our bedtime stories (*The Far Away Tree*, *Famous Five*, and fairy tales) and we'd listen to the *Story Teller* tapes. He took us on walks to the ancient graveyard down the road, where he'd tell us more stories. We frequently went to the hospital where Dad worked as a doctor, and at times, we went along on his house calls. We literally grew up in a hospital, which was actually a lot of fun.

In the mornings, Dad insisted we have Weet-Bix, Rice Bubbles, and hot milk for breakfast, which wasn't very nice. This was so we would not get sick from having cold milk in the Irish weather.

All in all, what I remembered was that we had a really great life that was happy and full of fun, and so it would seem. To people looking in, we were the perfect family: well-educated parents, middle-income earners, perfectly presented and well-mannered children, and on paper, it can really seem that way.

But what wasn't seen was the torment of emotional abuse, the terror of sexual abuse, or the destruction of alcoholism, which I was being forced to endure.

> It's truly scary what a little child's smile can hide and how much your imagination can become your escape.

CHAPTER 2

Sexual Abuse

THIS IS WHY I BECAME SO STAUNCH ABOUT NEVER HAVING children so that no one could ever hurt them. My belief is the safest place my babies can be is inside me, where no one can ever hurt them. I used to want to be like my mum and have eight children. I remember crying when I got my period for the first time, because it meant I could have babies—but that all changed.

I remember one day when I was polishing in my lounge room, I got to a picture sitting on the mantelpiece of myself and my brother posing for a school photo when I was about six years old. I suddenly began to cry inconsolably. I just kept saying to the little girl in the picture, over and over, 'You're okay, you're safe, you're okay. I've got you. Nobody's going to hurt you. You're safe, I've got you. You're safe, you're okay'. This went on for about half an hour. When I stopped crying and came to, I couldn't understand just what had happened or what that was about.

I only found out years later when the man himself told me, 'You would have been too young to remember. You would have been five or four or three. You would have been too young to remember'. What he meant was being sexually abused.

This explained why I was terrorised by people looking at me, or touching me, or having to lie down in front of people, or having my photo taken, even having to eat in front of people and put food in my mouth.

The thing is I don't have a working memory of what happened. It's been buried so deep. But what I do have is an emotional memory, terror and fears of people, places, situations, and times of day, things like being taken away from what I deem are my safe places.

When I bought my house, I couldn't drive over our bridge to go out of town to the next suburb because I didn't know what was there. I was thirty-two years old and I was too scared to drive over the bridge into the unknown because I was subconsciously afraid of being hurt.

When choosing my house, it was dictated by whether people could look in on me, either in the garden or through the windows, as it left me feeling too exposed, so I couldn't even consider the home to buy if they could.

To this day, I have rarely worn a swimsuit unless it's covered with shorts and a top. When in public I used to frantically pray, 'Please God, don't let them look at me, don't let them look at me, don't let them think bad things about me'.

And as I walked past certain types of men that subconsciously reminded me of him; the 'unsafe men'. (For me, there were the safe men, who reminded me of my brother, and then the unsafe men, who reminded me of him. My dad wasn't the sexual abuser, but it was my brother who made me felt safe).

I would use what I was carrying to cover my bust and then very awkwardly, I would swing it around to cover my back end so they couldn't see it as I walked away. If a man looked at me or seemed to come close, I would move or body block by putting my arm on my hip or my foot out or using my bag so there was distance between us. I've even used a shopping trolley in the supermarket when someone got too close by setting it in front of me.

I would scream when I went to the bathroom in my own home as a child or anywhere else I felt exposed, 'I'm in here! I'm in here! Don't come in! I'm in here! I'm in here'!

Change rooms were horrible. Those curtains that you can't close. Then having to spend ages tucking them in so you can't be seen and being in a panic that someone would walk in.

You see for me, men and bodies just meant I was to have sex and not in a good way—in an unwanted way. I used to feel like a sitting target and that at any moment it could happen again, and no one had a clue what I was going through.

I had a boyfriend for a short time and when he'd touch me, I just remember shaking. It was nothing to do with him. You see, I wanted a boyfriend, a husband, and a family, but my past memories didn't. He even asked me once, 'Why do you pull away when I go to kiss you'? I had no clue then. On one hand, I desperately wanted a boyfriend, really, I think, to validate me as a person because my self-esteem was shattered. On the other hand, I didn't because of my past hurt.

At times, I still oscillate with this, but I leave that in God's hands. If he wants a husband in my life, he can drop him at my front door; otherwise, I have no interest in looking. It's nothing against men. I actually really like men now, but once bitten, twice shy and it's just been a gradual work in progress being close to anyone let alone a man.

Even the thought of the honeymoon night makes me sick because people know what you are doing. And from a perspective of abuse, that's too much to bear; they may as well be watching. So, this is why it's in God's hands. If he asks that of me, I will walk that journey with him.

I remember my little nephew going to daycare for the first time. It took every ounce of restraint from me not to scream to his parents, 'Don't let him go, don't let him go'! It was the thought of his innocence being taken and being powerless to protect him from the world that had taken mine.

Sexual abuse has a ripple effect. It invades every aspect of your life and steals the very core of your being. For me, it stole my children and my husband, the ones I was meant to have. But even worse, it stole the life of my beautiful sister, when she took her life at age twenty-nine as a result of two men's abuse over a period of five years.

She had every medical treatment under the sun to deal with the effects of the abuse, which for her was self-harm, anorexia, bulimia, depression, and anxiety. But none of it could heal the wounds in her soul, and the flashbacks she was then experiencing were the devil's final blow.

When glimpsing through her journals, the depths of utter darkness that had taken over her soul was simply demonic. It was pure evil what Satan did to her. The lies that he convinced her of about who she was and her future were sickening. But the worst of all, that death was the only way to gain freedom from her pain.

I've experienced personally, and have seen in my sister, the depth of despair that the devil's lies can have over you and if it's in my power, I do not want anyone else to be trapped the way we were or to pay the ultimate price, as my beautiful sister did.

To this day, it has ripple effects on my family; it simply tore us apart. You see, she thought it would end her pain, but it just transferred it to us.

For me, bulimia started when I was fifteen years old and was taken by God when I was thirty years old. When one day, I realised what I was doing and I promised God that I would never do it again. I was tempted three times after that by the devil, but I resisted and never went back—ever.

It now disgusts me, even though I didn't know any better then, or how to stop it. I remain mortally ashamed of my behaviour because it was so wrong, both against God and myself.

These examples are a drop in the ocean of the daily impact this type of abuse has. The list can go on, but both time and that it's just too confronting won't allow me to share.

It doesn't talk either of feeling perpetually dirty and wanting desperately to be clean; believing you are so vulgar you smell; wanting your breasts to be removed so you don't get attention from men; the discomfort of having people standing close to you or giving them hugs in fear they think you want sex.

The constant worry that people will misinterpret your intentions of being friendly and loving for sexual desire, no matter if they are male or female. Believing there is something inside you, when in actual fact there is not—only the remnants of him.

So, you can imagine my terror when I became a nurse and had to see naked bodies, a constant reflection of my trauma and the very thing I was trying to escape, all the while, having to make the patient feel safe and secure while also providing dignity to them during their discomfort. Remember when I said it's scary what a smile can hide?

But, the thing is, Jesus came to set the captives free, which is just what he has been doing with me over the past thirteen years. Little by little and actually, day by day, he has been setting me free from the pain and torment of my past. But I've had to want it. I had to get to a stage that I was so desperate for change that when he called, I followed or more accurately, I very ungracefully stumbled along.

CHAPTER 3

Emotional Abuse

THERE IS ANOTHER TYPE OF ABUSE WHICH IS JUST AS SINISTER as sexual or physical abuse and that's emotional abuse. The fact is, every person has the ability to abuse. It is a conscious choice people make to hurt another person. When an abuser controls themselves in front of people they deem important but they do not with you, then there is your proof they are intentionally choosing to abuse you.

For me, I am not interested in discussing the people behind my abuse and I will attempt to disguise them as much as I can. My focus is to help you recognise signs of emotional abuse, understand that abuse is a choice, and understand how you can learn to manage an abuser but to do it with an attitude of love and forgiveness. Don't worry—I still find this hard, but it gets easier and it does work.

Remember, anything God asks of you is for the purpose of setting you free, and it will. Hate keeps you trapped, even when the person is out of your life. But love and forgiveness set you free from the continual pain of the abuse.

To forgive is to release our judgement of a circumstance to God, thereby trusting God to deal with it in his time and his way. This is one promise I held on to that: as I do my part, God does his. He says, 'For I the Lord love justice, I hate robbery and wrong, I will faithfully give them their recompense, and I will make an everlasting covenant with them'. (Isaiah 61:8 ESV) You see forgiveness is not about condoning bad behaviour; it's just not allowing it to continue poisoning you with hate.

But first, you must understand that there is an almighty spiritual war between God and Satan for your life. Satan's goal is to steal, kill, and destroy and he has a handful of ways to do this, and a primary one is through fear and by any means.

Think of something you are afraid of. How does it make you feel? Trapped, a prisoner, anxious, and powerless are a few descriptions. All through a little thing called fear, which uses its power to control your thoughts, feelings, and as a result your behaviour.

Now think of fear like a little puppet on the end of a string being controlled by its master. The little puppet's master is power and the string is the fear by which the little puppet is being controlled. When the master moves a string, the puppet has no choice but to move its arm or leg or dance around in obedience to the master's control, even if it doesn't want to.

Now, what if that little puppet was able to, one by one, cut the strings of fear? Then the master can no longer use its power to control the little puppet with fear and it becomes free. And yes of course, the little puppet gets to live happily ever after.

For me, I never knew or understood this. No one ever taught me how fear can be used to gain dominance, power, and control over you. Therefore, I want to share my experience with you in the hope of saving you time, heartache, frustration, and tears. I don't promise quick fixes to the changes you may want in your life but I am offering you the hope that with prayer, patience, and persistence, things can change.

This why my book is called *From Fear to Faith*. I absolutely despised myself as result of emotional and sexual abuse and lived in constant fear. So much so, that when I would have to speak to people, I would cover my mouth to prevent people hearing me. I had to communicate and be around people, but because of my fear, I was terrified of being heard. I wished I could have been swallowed up by the ground. So I would actually cover my mouth with my hand when I spoke. For me, it was agony to exist around people as people were simply the reflection of what I was not or more accurately, what I was made to believe I was not.

My self-hatred was to the point I believed that people couldn't tell if I was male or female. I believed I was so disgusting that I would hide my hands, in the fear that if people saw them, they would be convinced that I was a man when I was actually a girl. It's funny how God turns things around, because now my favourite body part is actually my hands.

This is what happens when Satan fills your mind with lies. You lose sight of who you actually are, where your worth and value come from, and what God says about you, which is that you are 'Precious in my eyes, and honoured, and I love you' (Isaiah 43:4 ESV) . You are 'Fearfully and wonderfully made' (Psalm 139:14 ESV). You are his child and he loves you so much that he died for you on the cross so that you could live.

But I didn't know this and became deceived because of all the lies I was being fed. You see, the devil is a master of deception. He's a liar and this is how he gets you enslaved by fear, making you trapped in a merry-go-round of terror and the belief that you can never get out. In fact, he convinces you that this is normal and that this is life. And sadly, if you're not taught any differently, that's where you remain unless you get set free.

But this is exactly where God comes into play, because he came to set the captives free that we may have life and have it abundantly and that is just what he has been doing for me.

Over the next chapters, I would like to give you some practical ways on how to recognise and manage abuse, but this is only the beginning of your journey to freedom.

I strongly recommend that you seek professional help for ongoing support and guidance. Then study more about abuse so that you can address your own unique situation. Make sure to pray constantly for wisdom, guidance, and protection, and for the right people to be put in your path to give you the right guidance and support.

Invading Your Territory

CHAPTER 4

Tactics

ABUSE IS AN INTENTIONAL BEHAVIOUR USED TOWARD ANOTHER person, animal, or object, intended to cause fear in order to gain complete dominance, power, and control.

In war, an enemy uses tactics to systematically attack their opponents, to destroy them, and gain the territory they want. They will seize as much territory as they can take until their enemies are utterly defeated and are rendered powerless.

When they gain the territory, they reign as a dictatorship not a democracy. Just think of governments throughout the world, past and present, and the difference between the ones reigning for the good of the people and the others reigning for power and dictatorship. Which worked and flourished where people felt safe?

You must learn to see abuse like this, as abusers use a set of tactics to steal your territory, to steal your freedom, to wear you down, and gain complete control over you. They will take you as a prisoner of war. You are then their slave and a personal trophy of their perceived dominance, power, and control.

But the absolutely wonderful thing is that when you understand their aim (which is to use *fear* to gain *dominance*, *power* and *control* over you) and then begin to understand the various tactics used to defeat you, you can then learn how to recognise and resist their attacks, which is how you fight back to regain your territory and regain your God-given freedom.

I liken it also to playing tennis. When they hit a ball at you (an attack), you just hit it right back. So then, their attacks become like water off a duck's back and they can no longer hurt you because they have lost their control over you, no matter what they try to do to you, all because you have taken back your power and regained control over your territory.

I had absolutely no understanding about this at all. I just knew I felt awful and was constantly in tears, afraid, and desperately wanting my life to change. I had even prayed and asked God to take the life of one of my abusers because I felt I couldn't take the pain any longer. After I had prayed this, I begged God to forgive me and told him I didn't want them dead; I just wanted my pain to stop.

I had no idea that my experience was actually abuse and that it was wrong. I just knew it as overwhelming pain. The sad thing was, that I had no idea that I had the very thing I needed to change my situation within me, until God began teaching me.

I am dumbfounded now at how controlled I was and how powerless I felt, like so many others.

The practical side of gaining back my territory and maintaining my freedom has been far from easy. At times, it has been very scary and overwhelming. But, my gradual freedom from fear and the process of maintaining it has been worth it.

I remember sitting at my desk one day thinking, *I feel like one of those women whose husband tells them what to eat, what to drink, what to wear, what to say, and who they can talk to.*

I remember having overwhelming anxiety when I had to speak to an abuser. Just the thought of telling them something or asking them a simple question had me physically shaking and hyperventilating to the point I was barely able to breathe as I spoke to them.

You see, I had pieces of the puzzle but had no picture to guide me with where they were to go, so I couldn't actually put the puzzle together. I didn't understand what the problem was or that the pieces were symptoms of abuse, and that they were related to how I was being treated or that it was even called abuse because I was never allowed to question it; I just had to accept how it was.

Then God began to show me information about domestic abuse, which was the missing piece I needed to begin putting the puzzle together. Through it, God began showing me that what I was experiencing had a name and it was called abuse. Then gradually, he has taught me how I could spot abuse and abusers and then how to counter their attack.

Every person's experience of abuse will be the same but different. I encourage you to research information on domestic abuse as a beginning to understand the abuse in your life. But remember, each experience is unique to the individual. Some areas will be more or less important to one person than another, and remember every abuser will use different tactics. It just depends on what they find works on you, what they can get away with, the relationship you have with them, and the environment (even the country) you are in.

As God began to give me the theory behind abuse, he showed me practically how it applied in my life. When I could not understand different aspects of it, I would ask and he would show me.

When you understand their tactics, you can understand your responses and then counter them so you do not fall into their trap. A bit like calming yourself down when you get distressed. You can learn to manage how you respond.

The following is my personal experience of God teaching me how to recognise abuse in my life and then how to manage it. I hope it begins to help you unlock yours.

CHAPTER 5

Wolf in Sheep's Clothing

BECAUSE ABUSE CAN BE HARD TO SPOT, I WANT TO GIVE A visual image of a wolf in sheep's clothing to make it easier to understand. Obviously, not everyone is an abuser, but the ones who are leave a trail of destruction.

Abusers are masters of disguise. A loving mother, devoted father, the trusted and loyal professional, such as a manager, coach, teacher, doctor, nanny, foster carer, nurse, or priest.

However, just because a person holds a certain position and says they will do the right thing does not mean they do. Therefore, always look for the evidence to support their claims. Never just assume, especially where children are involved. Importantly, always trust your gut instinct if something feels off.

God gave it to you for a reason, and that is all the evidence you or anyone else needs to keep vigilant if something does not seem right, even when you cannot put your finger on it.

Just think of Mother Teresa and Adolf Hitler. They were both kind and generous to those they loved and claimed to be doing good for humanity. Mother Teresa showed evidence by being a servant and actively loving others. But in contrast, Hitler murdered millions and was filled with hate.

This is why it gets so confusing in victims' and outsiders' heads. Abusers appear nice, helpful, hard-working, generous, charismatic, and even fighting for a cause. But you must look closely at the fruit their character produces, examine and test their behaviour and what they say over time.

Again, I want to reiterate why abusers are so sinister: they can love one person while murdering another. Remember, what they do behind closed doors will differ from what they do publicly as they are 'wolves in sheep's clothing'.

CHAPTER 6

Forcing and Faking Trust

AN OXYMORON, I KNOW, BUT I WANT YOU TO BE VERY CLEAR: it's not about earning or building your trust. It is a forced and fake trust that is all one-sided in an attempt to bait you, then trap you just like an animal. They intentionally lure you into a false sense of security through non-stop attention, compliments, and gifts. Then, bang—the trap door slams shut and you cannot get out. Their attention then turns to control, their compliments turn to criticism, and their gifts turn to punishment.

One of the experiences I had of this was at work with new staff on trial before getting their position. They appeared lovely and helpful, opening doors, carrying things, complimenting me for being supportive and on the job I was doing, asking questions, and seemingly being interested about my work and myself personally. But the reality was they were forcing and faking trust, gathering information, and sussing me out.

They changed topics when I would try to ask them the very questions they had asked me, only wanting my information but not willing to give me theirs. They subtly began telling me how they felt about people who got in their way, both privately and professionally, by telling me how they managed them, even how they got people fired.

They lured me in with a false sense of security, which then turned into a threat, after getting the position of 'I can get you fired'.

They had planted the seeds to later control my behaviour, so in the future, I would know the consequences to any actions they did not like. They had changed their behaviour when they got the security of the job, just like in a marriage. I had heard about people changing after they get married or moved to another country, and now I realised I had experienced it overtly at work.

Just like an animal lying in wait for its next meal, its prey unknowingly gets closer and closer while it patiently watches to anticipate their next move. Then bang they pounce and their prey is dead.

I realised the same thing also occurs in a more subtle, yet no less sinister, form when you start to stand up against an abuser. For a time, they may be seemingly nice to you, again, giving you a false sense of security, with a hope that they have changed and a belief that you were wrong, making you believe the abuse was not really that bad, and that you were overreacting.

But, the abuse then continues again and even gets worse because they feel a need to forge a stronger attack to keep you controlled.

This cycle keeps happening over and over and you eventually get weaker in your retaliation. They get stronger and you eventually have no more fight to give. And it's now just about surviving in the relationship and nothing more.

As children, we are taught stranger danger, but as adults, we are not taught relationship danger. Think of how abusers lure kids, forcing trust with nice things and promises. Then comes manipulation, guilt, and fear, then bam, they are trapped. We need to become aware of this in adult relationships, too.

This is why it is so important to test a person's character over a long period of time before getting into a relationship with them, and to observe how they speak about and treat others, because that's what they will do to you. Especially observe how they react when they get upset and things do not go their way.

Do not disclose personal details to people you just met. Just think of salespeople. They want and need your sale, so they work extra hard at being friendly, happy, positive, and polite just to sign you up. Then, if they are dodgy, they want nothing to do with you if there is a fault in their product, because they got what they wanted. It was never about you; it was always about them. Whereas a good company would bend over backwards to fix the fault to maintain their reputation and customer service. This is why I call it forcing and faking trust.

When buying a car, you ask and verify what it comes with. Then you take a test drive; do this with every person you come across. Ask yourself do they follow biblical principles of how to behave and treat others which are with love, joy, peace, patience, gentleness, goodness, kindness, faithfulness, and self-control.

Then look for the warning signs that it is a lemon, which is a dodgy car. Ask yourself, do they hold grudges? Are they unforgiving and merciless? Do they acknowledge when they do wrong and show remorse? Or do they always believe that they are right and the best? Can they genuinely empathise and care for others, including pets?

Do they have respect for others, their property and the authorities? How do they treat others who they feel are beneath them? Do not just take their word on how they describe themselves. Test their long-term behaviour and actions too. If what you see does not match what they say, get your boundaries up fast, because sadly, if they turn out be an abuser, this is how they will treat you.

My experience of abuse and abusers, at different levels, has been over forty-three years, anywhere from family, work, neighbours, strangers, and even friends. You see, when you are not taught what the trap of abuse looks like, you just keep walking into it. You are blind to it, so it makes you a sitting duck for anyone with abusive behaviour, no matter how small or brief the interaction.

I really want people to understand that abuse is not isolated either. It is not sexual abuse, domestic abuse, elder abuse, school or workplace bullying, war, terrorism, or dictatorship. It's all the same thing; it's all abuse. It is one person or persons using fear to gain dominance, power, and control over another. And it's not just men towards women. Over half of my abusers were women who, in my experience, were worse than the men.

Depending on the environment and if it is permitted, it can become the culture and the norm, either within a family, workplace, community, nation, or country.

I am now wary of overzealous, complimentary, gift-giving people who smother me and demand constant contact, and expect my personal life be an open book to them—people who ask me to keep their secrets and keep me as their confidant.

I move cautiously around them to test their actual motives toward me to see if it is just their personality or if there are other warning signs of abuse.

I set clear boundaries that I control who has the right to be in relationship with me and that no one can have it without permission. I don't ingratiate them because they give me gifts or compliments and I limit how much I will say about my personal life and the contact I have with them. Realise if someone gives you a gift, you do not owe them anything in return. If it was genuine and from the heart, they won't expect it.

CHAPTER 7

Removing Boundaries

BOUNDARIES ARE WHERE YOU END AND ANOTHER PERSON begins. It's the personal, physical, and mental space that separates you from the next person. Boundaries give you your own unique identity and existence, separate from others. It is a protective barrier that keeps you safe from others. Just like your skin, it is your first line of defence against abuse.

The problem with abuse is that your boundaries get removed and you never even knew they existed or that you had the right to have them. The abuser does not want you to be separate from them; they want you to be theirs alone and at any cost.

Your boundaries become eroded like a rotten piece of wood when your self-esteem has been systematically desecrated by an abuser. This is why abusers can walk all over you, and this process is done in many ways.

For me, a healthy self-esteem and our boundaries are two in one. God has shown me that he has to deal with one to restore the other. When you have a healthy self-esteem, you are able to recognise what is or isn't acceptable behaviour toward you. And then you can respond accordingly to set your boundaries.

An example of how self-esteem and boundaries impact each other was when I would walk on a foot path. If anyone came toward me, I would automatically get off the footpath and give them all the room. Then when they had passed me, I got back on the path. My self-esteem was so low that I did not feel worthy to walk equally with anyone. I would let them walk past so they did not have to consider me and move.

God began challenging me about this by making me walk on the footpath while someone else was on it. It was so hard that, to stop myself jumping off the footpath, so that they did not have to move over to make equal way for me, I literally had to stop and stand still until they walked past me. It was incredibly uncomfortable to actually stand my ground as they went by. Now, for the most part, I have no problem standing my ground to be treated equally, as it is my God-given right.

Just like the footpath, I remember when God was teaching me that I had the right to use the voice he had given me to speak my opinion. That statement itself is loaded with freedom that I never knew was my right to have.

God started to show me other people speaking up for themselves and giving their opinion without retracting it if the other person disapproved. I was utterly baffled when I saw people being forthcoming, direct, and unapologetic with their opinions. It was truly baffling to me.

They not only said their opinion, but they believed they had a right to it and, they were totally unapologetic for it.

Initially, I saw this as forceful and domineering, but it wasn't. It is actually a person's right to be able to express their opinion in a respectful and honest way to assert their boundaries. In the Bible, it's called speaking the truth in love.

To this day, it is still a work in progress, which God is little by little working out with me. At the moment he has been getting me to express my opinion to the very people I have been most afraid of! But it is a lesson I have to pass to gain total freedom from the power of abuse.

It's not our right to disregard or disrespect the opinion of another even if we disagree with them. They also have the right to speak. But the problem I experience is that people, for different reasons, feel they have to attack the other person to make them back down from expressing their opinion. They are afraid that if someone does not agree with them, they will be seen as wrong and lose power or control.

I've even experienced that even if I share the very same opinion as an abuser, because they don't want me to have an opinion or a voice and in turn express my independent thoughts. They actually say, 'No, no, that's not right', then they say the very thing I had just said, simply reframed. You see, it wasn't what I said. It was that I said something, that I spoke my opinion, which is what they don't want you to do.

The more you speak your opinion, the stronger your self-esteem and boundaries become, and the more independent you are from the abuser, which causes them to lose control over you. Then, when someone else hears and agrees with you, it validates your opinion and independent judgement, causing you to be even more confident in speaking your opinion. You then become even more independent of an abuser, and they do not want that under any circumstance.

This is when abuse becomes very dangerous. If an abuser realises they are losing dominance, power, and control over you, they will up their attack on you in any way they can.

This, horrifically, is what can lead to victims of domestic abuse being killed or injured, and why it is so critically important to immediately get professional help when you realise you are in an abusive situation to find a way to safely manage getting out of it.

Conquering Your Territory

CHAPTER 8

Approval

ABUSERS SYSTEMATICALLY ERODE YOUR SELF-ESTEEM THROUGH their tactics, and thereby your self-confidence, causing you to be completely dependent on them and others for approval. This is because your self-esteem is how you perceive yourself and your self-confidence is how you walk in that perception.

Approval is then like an accelerator in a car: when you have it and keep getting it, this builds your self-esteem and you become more confident in what you think, say, and do. You then become less dependent on others for their approval because that now comes from within you.

A bit like this: when you have a healthy self-esteem, you are like a child on a tricycle. You feel stable as you ride along. But when they first go on a two-wheel bike, they are uncertain, scared, wobbly, and can't go very far. That's akin to a low self-esteem.

A healthy self-esteem is having the ability to back yourself and not require approval from others. You may seek validation to confirm your ideas but do not require their approval. Low self-esteem is having a dependence on others to back you through their approval. This renders you powerless and very vulnerable because you are constantly looking for approval from others. Sadly, you can be willing to do anything to get it and keep it when you are in a constant state of self-doubt. This is why a healthy self-esteem is vital in life.

Now the flip side, of course, is that some people like being dependent and saved by others. But that is a whole other kettle of fish because they are choosing not to take responsibility for themselves. It suits them to let others take control, even if they cry out, 'Poor me'. That's a whole other type of person, who can get you by trapped if you are a rescuer, which people with low self-esteem can become to get approval.

Therefore, if you don't know who you are as a child of God, that you are precious because your worth and value are in him, then anything you are told by an abuser will be absorbed by you and become your reality. Abusers will actually paint a completely distorted picture for you to look at and believe as your reality about yourself, other people, and your life. And because you do not know any difference, you will believe it.

I would continuously recite a mantra to myself that was belittling, berating, and self-deprecating. I was so programmed to believe that my existence was despised that this is how I spoke to myself repeatedly. It was to the point that I didn't even have to say the words; a simple glance in the mirror dissolved me into tears because of my own self-hatred.

Unfortunately, most of you will understand what I mean, and this is what really upsets me. I want you to know you don't have to think this way about yourself. Yes, I just put the responsibility on you. But, that with a healthy, biblically based self-esteem, what others say to you is cross checked by what God says, both to you and about you.

I was going to a gathering once where an abuser was giving me the silent treatment. I could not understand why it was upsetting me so much. I knew their behaviour was wrong towards me and they had no right to treat me this way. But I could not get out from their hold over me and the feeling of being inferior.

When I asked God, he showed me I was waiting for their approval and that if they spoke to me, I would feel as if I was pardoned and exonerated by them even though I had done nothing wrong, just like a child, waiting to see whether their parents will be upset at them and are only relieved when they see they are not.

God taught me that his is the only approval I need to be concerned about and if I am following him and not sinning against my conscience, then I have no reason to be concerned.

A lady came to my house for the first time and I began to get worried about what she would think of my home. You see, I had renovated my house, and it was my design ideas that I feared would not be approved. So I had to go back to God and rationalise this fear with him. Through this, he reminded me that my approval is from him not man. In the end, as soon as she walked in, she stated, 'This is a beautiful home'. I had immediate relief, giving thanks to God for the reassurance and for building my confidence with the decisions I had made.

God has so much to tell you in the Bible about your worth, value, and the future he has for you, not to mention the minor fact that even when we fell short of doing the right thing, he still loved you and I so much that he gave his life in exchange for ours. So what does that say to you about how precious you are to him? Unlike an abuser, you don't continuously have to gain God's approval. You were already freely given it at the beginning of time. You just have to receive it, not earn it.

CHAPTER 9

Criticism

> Death and life are in the power of the tongue (Proverbs 18:21 ESV)

CRITICISM AND PRIDE ARE RED FLAGS TO ABUSE. ABUSERS WILL tear you down while building themselves up, either directly or indirectly. This is how abusers conquer your territory. Be aware of someone who is constantly criticising others when you first meet them, as they will later be doing it to put you down so they feel on top, and that's wrong.

You can build up or tear down other people, which is an abuser's aim. Like water torture, criticism is a constant drip that wears you down. Unfortunately, you will eventually believe just what you were taught to believe if you are not aware of this tactic.

I was criticised simply for a pair of shoes I chose to wear; mocked and laughed at because I started knitting; laughed at because of the colour of a flower pot in my garden; and mocked because of how I ran while exercising. They criticised me for my weight, the length of my toenails, the style of my hair, and the fact I had pale skin, making me go outside once to get a suntan with no sun cream, which resulted in a first-degree burn requiring a trip the doctor.

I was verbally abused when I refused to buy them cigarettes and confronted their alcoholism, amongst other things. Abusers can never let you be right as it undermines their authority over you. It is exhausting always being beaten down simply for existing.

Once as a child, while visiting a family friend who had recently had a baby, I remarked that the baby was sucking its thumb, which it was. However, I was swiftly told, 'Don't say that'. I was scolded when a girl in a cafe went to the fridge and got a drink without asking her parent, who did not mind. However, I was scathingly told, 'Don't you ever do that'.

The sad thing was that I had just won at an eisteddfod and we went to a cafe to have a nice lunch, yet I was being abused for something another girl did.

An abuser was two rooms away from me and they were making very loud sighing noises as they watched TV. I was trying to sleep, so I got up, went to their room, and asked if they could keep the noise down. No sooner had I left their room had they dramatically increased the volume of their sighs as punishment. I lay in bed and sobbed myself to sleep while they intentionally and dramatically sighed loudly.

I would get scolded for trying to empathise if an abuser was upset only to be scathingly told, 'You do not understand'! So, I remember consciously changing what I was saying to try and prevent an attack. Like dodging landmines, you are cautious about where you tread in an attempt not to set them off. The problem is they are seemingly hidden and unpredictable and you never know when they might explode, only that they will. As a result, you learn to wait to be told what you can do or say.

In high school, I remember waiting in line to ask my teacher a question. Other children just went ahead of me as I stood there for ages. Eventually, my teacher became frustrated that others were going ahead of me, through no fault of their own, and called me up so I could have my turn.

Just think of a dictator in a country. When people speak, it is in submission to the leader. It is never freely or they would be punished. Well, that is the same thing in abuse, making it hard to spot. People seem free when they speak, but really they are not as they are under the watchful eye of their abuser.

Everything you say and do is criticised because that's how they erode your self confidence in your own judgement and opinion, to condition you, like training a dog, but again, they get the treats. So, then you always ask them if what you think is okay and you stop using your own thoughts because you will get criticised. But, you do not realise it as that; you just blame yourself, believing you are daft and insane and that no one likes you.

They make sure you never trust your own judgement, which was another reason why writing this book has been so hard, fighting the belief that I am insane and that I am completely wrong.

The perpetual record of, 'You're insane. If anyone knew what you were thinking, you would be locked in a mental hospital for life'—I can't tell you how hard God has had to fight this off me. This war within me, of desperately wanting to write my book to help others, but having an overwhelming fear of self-exposure. But, that's where trust in God's leading comes in. As the Bible teaches, what the devil meant for my harm, God will use for my good.

Not long ago, I was going home on the train and the abuse was very bad. I told God that I could not fight any longer. I told the devil he had won and I gave up. I had nothing left to give in the fight. I then sat beside a scruffy young man who asked how I was. I replied, 'Not great'. Then I asked how he was, which led to him telling me about the physical, sexual, financial, and emotional abuse he had experienced in his family and from his ex-partner.

I shared parts of my experience and how God had been helping me through abuse, and how wrong what he experienced was and how sorry I was for him. At my stop, as we said good bye, this young man jumped up, thanking me with a bear hug. Then he kept eagerly smiling and waving me good bye. I left reignited with a hope that maybe I'm not insane, and maybe I can help. So God has just kept pushing me forward, and this is just how God works, putting what you need, where you need it and when you need it.

But, that's the agony of abuse: you have this world of trauma within yet you have to exist. You have to go to school, and work, and do life as normally as you can. For me it resulted in a perpetual record in my head of *You're a liar.* Because anything I said was twisted and told was wrong. You simply could never have an opinion; it was beaten out of you, and the only thing I knew was everyone thinks I am wrong and a liar.

If I ever said anything and someone gave the slightest evidence of what I perceived was disapproval, I would literally jump back in a panic, retract what I said and gush with apologies and explanations in order to restore their approval of me.

Going to the doctor was horrid. With this in my head, it was agony. They are an intellectual authority, so it was a double whammy of them thinking you are a liar and daft, too. That was nothing to do with them; they were always lovely. But that's how you were programmed: to see yourself the way the abuser describes you and then you exist believing that's how the world views and sees you.

Recently God gave me a beautiful realisation: that as my self-esteem has been growing, my need for approval has been decreasing. I no longer grovel desperately for approval by trying to explain or justify myself when someone says something I perceive to be critical of me. God has been teaching me that I don't have to justify everything I say or do with an explanation to other people, as long as I can justify myself to God.

CHAPTER 10

Expressionless When Speaking to You

When an abuser is being expressionless as they are speaking to you, it erodes your self-esteem and confidence. It raises self-doubt and you are made to question what you say, think, and do because you are not given the validation and approval that results in your confidence being built when engaging in a conversation with them. It is also another clever tactic, bit like intentionally yawning while you speak.

You then try and make up for their silence, like a dog jumping higher and higher to get their treat. Fumbling your words, you renege the question you asked, the opinion you gave, or the statement you made in the hope of getting a response that shows their approval.

You lose confidence and doubt yourself, leaving you scared and less likely to approach them again. It renders you weak, anxious, intimidated, and dependent on them for any snippet of approval and at any cost. Either physically, mentally, emotionally, sexually, or financially, you become their slave.

We coo at babies and animals, and have high-pitched voices to resonate our approval and give encouragement. We over animate our expressions to encourage them, showing our support and approval. However, abusers intentionally withhold love, affection, attention, validation, approval, and encouragement in a bid to snuff out your fire, your passion, your personality, your potential, and, ultimately, your confidence.

It was horrifying when I realised that this was happening—that someone meant to love me was actually intentionally hurt me. To this day, I still cannot understand this mindset. But the great thing is that these patterns of behaviour get easier to spot when you learn them. Then with God, you can fight back and resist any attack on your freedom.

The flip side of this is that they can do the very opposite to deflect responsibility and your concerns with distracting theatrics, overly dramatic reactions, gestures, and expressions, yelling, even storming off, becoming physical, or threatening to harm themselves or others.

Like a child having a tantrum to get what they want, they know you will do whatever it takes to settle them down, even taking the blame, which is how they divert having to take responsibility or accountability for the concerns you raised. They use what they can to block you from regaining your territory and lure you back under their control.

To hunt a fish, you don't use a machete; you use a net, spear, or fishing rod. Just as the weapon you choose depends on what you are hunting, abusers will use whatever weapon they can that will work on you. Some victims are easy to catch; others are harder. Some try to fight back and some won't.

CHAPTER 11

Rejection

VALIDATION, ACCEPTANCE, AND APPROVAL IS WHAT EVERYONE craves. Therefore, abusers make sure nothing, nothing, nothing you ever do will be good enough for them. They have to keep you down to stop you rising up in every aspect of your relationship. They do not respect equality; they only respect their own dominance, power, and control over others.

Therefore, rejection is another way abusers render you powerless by simply snuffing you out. Like a fire doused in water, without oxygen there is no flame. Very similar to the silent treatment and being expressionless just on a different slant and slightly more cunning. It is done through devaluing your existence just by ignoring you or dismissing what you say or do.

As part of their rejection tactics, denying and minimising are used to undermine your expressed concerns or comments, to make you doubt yourself, renege your remarks and actions, to make you take the blame and for them to avoid taking responsibility for their behaviour.

'I did not say that', 'That's not true', or 'You're exaggerating' makes you doubt yourself and makes you question your own judgement. They can be scarily calm and controlled so you look hysterical and emotional when they respond like this. Then you begin to question everything you think, say, or do, forcing you to only follow and trust the abuser because they appear to have proven your judgement cannot be trusted.

I know for me, I kept looking for patterns to keep the abuser happy, but the goal post always changed no matter how hard I tried. I came to realise that they will never let what you do be good enough because it keeps you fearful, on edge, and trying to please them. You can never relax. If they give you approval, they lose power and they'll never do that.

The heart of what abusers do is reject. All human beings want validation, acceptance, and approval. So, we will do what is necessary to maintain it, just so we can be part of the pack. Just think of peer pressure with children uncertain of themselves and wanting to fit in.

This is why teaching children about biblical principles and God's commandments is so important, so they will have a strong foundation of what is or is not acceptable behaviour toward themselves and others. When this comes into question, they will know the answer and what to do. Like road rules, if you don't know them, how do you know what is or is not safe to do?

Abusers make sure they disapprove of you. That is why understanding that God not only approves of you, but that he does so, while you are still a sinner is so important, meaning, he knows you're not perfect, he knows you make mistakes. He knows you're human, and not a robot. But he absolutely loves you anyway, so much that he actually died for you even though you are in that state.

He loves you just as you are this second and you are already accepted and approved by him. You are already enough. That's what motivates you as Christian to follow the Bible. Because he loves you so much, you want to do things his way because you can see it is not to hurt you but to love and protect you.

Reigning in Your Territory

CHAPTER 12

Removing Your Opinion

EVERYONE HAS A RIGHT TO THEIR OWN OPINION, BUT NO ONE has the right to harm another because they have a difference of opinion. It's such a basic thing really. It's what you like or do not like, what you prefer and what you don't. It's your own personal thoughts on a matter, and your right to express them, and have them received respectfully.

Therefore, you having an opinion, let alone sharing it, is dangerous for an abuser. It makes you a threat even though it is not your intention. They take it as a personal attack because they live in constant combat, always fighting to be on top.

Instead of being able to respect another person's right to their opinion, they have to either make you submit, back down, keep quiet, or agree with them, like keeping a muzzle or a leash on you. All through threats, intimidation and manipulation.

Because they cannot tolerate perceived criticism, they will attack, just like an animal. They do what they feel they need to keep you down, and especially from speaking out against their abusive behaviour. Having an opinion makes you independent of them and can show up their flaws, weaknesses, and wrong behaviour, which they do not want to be accountable for. And it reduces their power over you, making you dangerous to them because they lose their control over you.

This sounds strange, but it was only about a year ago that God gave me the revelation that I have a voice. Although I could speak and did, I did not use my own internal voice or opinion out of fear. It sounds so silly, but I didn't realise this, because to have a voice, you have to have an opinion. And when most of your life, you have been told that you have no opinion or your opinion is wrong or insane, then mocked and continuously nitpicked, you cease to have a voice of your own or remember you have one. You just follow and agree with what you are told, even when you disagree, because the fight is just too hard. It is exhausting being beaten down just because you try and express an opinion.

You see, you wait for permission, you wait to be told, and you wait to know what you are allowed or not allowed to say or do. Otherwise, there are consequences. This has a severe impact on your ability to trust your own judgement or express it, because your confidence is greatly diminished as you believe one thing yet are told another. And eventually, you lose all trust in yourself, your own judgement, and your ability to make and hold decisions because your confidence has been eroded.

Abuse is snide, cunning, subtle, and hidden. Abuse is not public. It is deceptive, as they disguise it, even from the victim, which is why it's so insidious. Abusers convince you their behaviour is love, and they are right and you are always wrong, which is why you end up feeling insane. You become so confused about what reality is, because you keep getting told that what you think is reality is actually not reality.

They reflect everything you do, say, think, and feel in a distorted way, which is why your head can feel like a washing machine.

You just do not know which way is up as you have lost your perception of reality. Like those fun house mirrors at a circus, the reflection you see is completely warped. And because that is all you are allowed to see of yourself, then that is what you believe.

That's why reading the Bible daily is so important: to reboot you back to the reality of what God says about you and how he sees you, which is through a lens of love. You are so precious to him that he gave is life in exchange for yours. That's how much he loves you, which is a far cry from the so-called love of an abuser.

They use this kind of tactic in torture. They make you confess something that you know is not true by savagely torturing you to the point of exhaustion and near death. Sound familiar? Abusers then stick a label on it, and call it love, and call you insane. I call it *sick*.

Because of this, I became highly anxious, constantly apologising and justifying myself when I would speak. I was consumed with self-doubt, always trying to please and appease others, and constantly needing reassurance that I was doing the right thing. I was always doing things to make others happy, even when detrimental to myself and all for fear of disapproval. Just think of how timidly abused animals behave compared to ones who were not.

As a result, although I am an adult and a nurse, I have been terrified of certain levels of responsibility. I am really only comfortable when I have someone senior that I can cross check my decisions with, even though I am competent. I think I am one of the few people who has no problem taking orders from a doctor.

However, like with everything, God is slowly healing this area of my life. But it takes time to rebuild confidence in your own judgement and the ability to question the judgement of others.

CHAPTER 13

I Don't Want to Argue

THE STATEMENT USED BY ABUSERS OF, 'I DON'T WANT TO ARGUE' can be translated as, 'I'm not discussing this with you', which is a tactic used by abusers to block you from speaking and having a voice.

It undermines and eliminates your opinion, making you speechless and powerless, then falsely shames you into not giving your opinion again. You do so only when you have been given their permission.

It falsely makes them out to be the better person, when in reality, it is a tactic used to block you from freely expressing your opinion and sharing in an equal balance of power in the relationship. It keeps them in control over you, stopping your concerns from being addressed, or them taking responsibility.

I literally learnt this lesson one week ago. It is literally used to shut the conversation down, which means your concerns are not addressed. No different to the silent treatment and ignoring you. At times, I have had to stop conversations, even relationships, but this was to protect myself from abusive behaviour, not to control others, which goes back to having boundaries and your motivation.

CHAPTER 14

Speaking on Your Behalf

I have had abusers literally speaking on my behalf. For example, when I was directly asked questions, they actually replied for me, again rendering me powerless and making me speechless.

I was at a gathering once where my abuser kept blocking my ability to answer questions that a newcomer was directly asking me in order to get to know me. Eventually, I got up and said, 'You clearly don't need me to answer questions', then I left the conversation.

I had an abuser redirect phone calls at work so I could not be involved in various decisions needing to be made. They even told me to go to them first, if I wanted to talk to a person that I needed to liaise with, stating that they would speak with the person on my behalf. These tactics are used to empower them and disempower you.

I now try to ensure one person doesn't get to dominate a conversation by being intentional when talking to people in a group through reading the signs and being aware of opportunities to reinforce someone's opinion who may be getting spoken over when they give it. This is especially important with children to make them feel safe and confident to speak up by validating them when they do.

CHAPTER 15

Involving Another Person or Persons

ONE TACTIC ABUSERS USE IS INVOLVING ANOTHER PERSON OR persons as their defence and reinforcement when you try to express your opinion. This tactic plays on your fear of what others will think of you and what you already think of yourself, like when an abuser threatened to go to my work to say malicious things about me. Family and relatives were regularly used as a threat by one of my abusers.

Involving others is a way to undermine you in an attempt to weaken your stance on an opinion. It's a threat and manipulation. 'If you don't back down and get back in line, I will get someone else to prove you are wrong and I am right. I will expose your deepest fears and shames to them and embarrass and humiliate you to ensure you never speak up again. I will publicly shame you'.

But the things is, we all have shames and regrets. That is why it is important to confess them to God and receive his forgiveness, so they can no longer have a hold on you, like me with this book. I have exposed my deepest shames to the world. But I had to come to a place of acceptance, so they cannot be held against me.

When involving others, abusers can threaten to call authorities to have your children taken away. They threaten children with being taken away by authorities when they speak up. They can threaten to call your family, friends, or your work. Anyone they think you will be afraid of, intimidated by, or feel ashamed in front of if they were told what the abuser is threatening to tell them, whether it is true or not. Like when parents say to their children, 'If you don't do this, I'll tell your teacher' or 'If you're not good, Santa won't come'.

Again it is all a threat and manipulation to make you behave the way they want you to, by making you afraid, enabling them to keep the power over you and to control you by weakening your defence and strengthening theirs.

However, the difference is that you are an adult not a child and they have no right to threaten, intimidate or manipulate you. They cannot remove your right to freely express an opinion or raise concerns when there is problem that you want to address. Remember, abusers do not want you to have a voice at all costs.

And remember this: we are all human, therefore, we all sin and fall short of the glory of God. So if he forgives us when we genuinely repent of our sins and ask for his forgiveness no matter how bad our sin, then we should not fear what abusers try to hold over us or what others think.

CHAPTER 16

Unpredictable

UNPREDICTABILITY IS SUCH A BIG THING IN ABUSE, NEVER knowing when they are going to go off or what will set them off. Their constant threats, intimidation and physical manipulation means you can never feel safe. You are always on edge, whether you are conscious of this or not. You become very vigilant for danger, for signs they are about to erupt, and you then try your best to stop it happening at all costs.

Because their abusive behaviour is not based on rational logic, you have no pattern to follow, which is why it is so hard; what appeased them last time doesn't necessarily work the next time. So you are always on edge because it seems there is nothing you can do to stop it. This fear then filters into every other area and relationship of your life. You very quickly become highly anxious, hyper-vigilant, and a people pleaser, doing what you can to keep people happy.

This made working and being around people really hard for me. As you are responsible to speak up, but internally it terrifies you because you know that speaking up can cause swift punishment. You then try to gauge how people will respond to you in any given situation.

You are on constant guard for signs of disapproval in an attempt to undo whatever you felt caused it, before their abuse is triggered. A bit like trying to figure out which wire to cut before the bomb explodes.

For me, it has been the biggest difficulty gauging responses and trusting my own judgement, even when I know I am correct. The constant overthinking and worrying that what you say, do, or think is not only wrong but that there will be consequences really is exhausting. I have come a long way, but I am still growing in this area.

CHAPTER 17

Isolating You

ABUSERS WILL DO ALL SORTS OF THINGS TO ISOLATE YOU OUT of their jealously and belief that you are their possession, which you are not; it is a privilege to be in relationship with you, not their right to own you.

Abusers will do anything to isolate you and limit your contact with others because to them, you are their possession and no one else's. This is why it is so sickening for precious little children. They are so defenceless and have no power to protect themselves. It's horrifying how abusers treat these little ones. It's terrifying what happens behind closed doors to them. Even worse, they are made to believe this is love, and this is what God is like, and that you are punished just for existing.

Abusers will return home late so you can no longer go out to see your friends, family, church, or doctors, or keep other appointments. They even stop you from working but make it sound like it's for your own good. They like you to only be focused on them, so they have to eliminate or reduce your access to others by not allowing you to do activities away from them or without them.

This can come across as them being loving and kind. But when you assess their pattern, they will make sure others aren't involved. It's only you and them. They isolate you from the herd, which makes you more vulnerable and an easier prey to break down and control. Like a kingdom being divided, it's easier to conquer.

They go so far as to split you from people you are close to. They will convince you to move towns, even countries, to cut ties with any of your supports. They stop your phone calls or means to make contact. Systematically, they will make you believe lies about those you love: 'That person's insane' or 'They only want your money'. They plant seeds of doubt in your mind about your loved one's intentions. And it can be the very thing they themselves are doing to you, such as having affairs.

They tell you lies about the people in your life so that you don't trust them or fear them. So gradually, you separate from them, which gives abusers a stronger hold on you. It means there is less of a chance of someone else speaking into your life and getting you help.

Isolation is one of the scariest aspects of abuse because you have no other sounding board. Everything they say about you, the world, and your future becomes all you know.

A friend called while I was a passenger in the car with an abuser. The abuser couldn't handle that my attention was elsewhere. So they carried on having an entire conversation at me while I was trying to talk to my friend, forcing me to terminate the phone call. Then the abuser stopped talking at me because they no longer had to fight for my attention; I was all theirs. They will do all sorts of things to stop you contacting others.

I had to organise a youth group once. Because I was making phone calls and making friends, I was banned from making the calls under the guise that it cost too much. So I got my own phone line hooked up into the house, which I paid for. But it was removed and I was blocked from making calls. So it was evident that it was not to do with the cost, but retaining power and control by blocking me from building relationships with others.

When eating out, if the focus was not on the abuser, they would literally huff and puff, sulk, and be angry until you put all the focus back on them, just like a child having a tantrum. It's exhausting, because if you don't lavish them with undivided attention, it will cost you in some way.

Along with the isolation, there is no privacy from an abuser. You are under constant watch, like a prisoner in a cage never able to roam free. They are very possessive. Asking others about you, monitoring your calls, what you do and who you speak to, where you go, and going through your property. There is no privacy or personal space.

You are terrified of breathing without their permission. And you are a nervous wreck, yet you can't understand why. Now that you are isolated, you are dependent on them, so you become trapped and unable to cry out for help.

Why? Because isolation renders you totally dependent on them to think for you and you must wait for their approval. It gives them full control. If they destroy your ability to have trust and confidence in yourself and then others, then they know you won't move away from them.

[illegible] looked [illegible] the noise, which [illegible] around and two [illegible] and [illegible] gas [illegible] It was evident that [illegible] the cast [illegible] power and [illegible] from [illegible] swimmers.

[illegible] out, [illegible] was [illegible] would [illegible] and [illegible] until you [illegible] the [illegible] just [illegible] a tantrum [illegible] because [illegible] visit [illegible] who [illegible] you [illegible] some [illegible]

[illegible] the [illegible] an [illegible] never able [illegible] They are very [illegible] Adults [illegible] and [illegible] cats [illegible] would [illegible] where [illegible] through [illegible] Their [illegible] privacy [illegible]

[illegible] ones. And you [illegible] and [illegible] that [illegible] them [illegible] one [illegible] for help [illegible]

May [illegible] you [illegible] must [illegible] the [illegible] It was [illegible] to have [illegible] yourself and then others, that they know you won't move away from them.

Restoring Your Territory and Freedom

CHAPTER 18

Restoring Your Territory Physically and Emotionally

YOU NEED TO REGAIN YOUR PHYSICAL, EMOTIONAL, MENTAL, and spiritual strength to be able to restore your territory. You can achieve nothing when you are exhausted, let alone freedom. When sediment settles in water, then there is clarity. Similarly, you need to rest and recharge so you can refocus and find clarity.

Do not get overwhelmed and expect everything to change in a day. Let God lead you. There have been enough rules and regulations put on you, but God is not like that. Remember, he is gentle and kind, tender hearted, and full of mercy—the things your abuser is not. He doesn't demand perfection; he just wants obedience to his promptings.

When he prompts you to go to bed and not stay up late, then go. If he prompts you to exercise, like taking a walk, or encourages you to see a friend, then do it. He cares just as much about you physically, emotionally, and mentally as he does spiritually. Remember, he created you both inside and out.

Get proper sleep, rest, and relaxation. Eat a healthy diet, drink water, and exercise as you are able. Make an appointment to see your doctor for professional help and referrals. Have a well-balanced routine, both daily and weekly. If you are using drugs or cigarettes, or have an alcohol or other addiction, get professional help to get off them. Reconnect with supportive family, friends, and community or church groups.

These are the foundations to help restore and maintain your strength. Without regaining physical and emotional strength, you will not have the mental strength or emotional stability to restore your territory and maintain your freedom.

God did this with Elijah the prophet. He wanted to commit suicide after fighting a war due to utter exhaustion. So God made him eat, rest, and sleep three days to regain strength. You can't use willpower when you have been depleted physically and emotionally. Yes, God gives us special times of grace, but we are still human beings in human bodies so look after them and build a strong foundation.

Simply start with a prayer by asking God to help and guide you on how to do this in your own unique situation. If you are currently in an abusive relationship, this will be a mountainous task on your own.

But remember that you are not expected to recover alone or all at once. God is there to help, so ask him and you will be amazed at what he does for you. Just make sure to follow his lead when he gives you that gentle nudge.

CHAPTER 19

Restoring Your Territory Mentally

RESTORING YOUR TERRITORY MENTALLY IS ABOUT LEARNING as much as you can about abuse and how to manage it safely. Then study and understand the tactics your abuser uses toward you, which will help you to counter them, either directly or indirectly, with your response.

Remember, safety is your first priority. When they realise you are taking back your territory, their aggression *will* increase toward you and your loved ones. This is why you must get professional support for guidance with your unique situation.

This is terrifying. Believe me—I know! I don't want to scare you. I'm just trying to prepare you so you do not respond impulsively thinking, *Bless God, they have no right to treat me like this.* Yes, this is true, but they don't care. They only care about themselves and their dominance over you and at any cost. They do not see the world as you do. Just remember Hitler; he was ruthless and merciless, yet he was a human being, too. So you *must* carefully plan and prepare your steps to freedom with professional support, and always put your safety first.

As a Christian, I hold beliefs that are different to those of non-Christians. And the reality is there are many countries where Christians are persecuted for their beliefs, which I have experienced personally.

This was something I wrestled with for a long time when deciding to write this book. I wanted to help others to be free from abuse but knew there could be personal a cost because, in this modern world, it is not popular to hold Christian beliefs.

But this is where faith and courage come in. I don't know how this book will be received. Frankly, it could be highly criticised in certain arenas because it's from a Christian perspective, but this is where the rubber hits the road for me.

I can spend the rest of my life fearing the persecution and criticism of others because I am openly sharing my belief about God in my life and how he saved me from abuse. But if I did that, I'd just be a hypocrite who hasn't actually gone from fear to faith. I would be loving God privately but too afraid to talk about him publicly.

So, I choose not to be a hypocrite. I choose not to be controlled by fear, and I choose to use my voice to express my opinion in the hope of freeing others trapped in abuse.

You see, I can't separate anything in my life from God; it's all him. I know that apart from him, I can do nothing and I am completely fine to accept that. I don't need personal praise because I have experienced how little I can achieve on my own and experienced what can happen with God at my side.

My point being that there is a cost to restoring and maintaining freedom from abuse. You will have to decide for yourself the price you are able and willing to pay and when.

CHAPTER 20

Restoring Your Territory Spiritually

STUDY THE BIBLE; THERE IS NO WAY AROUND IT. YOU CANNOT change what you do not know to change. People building flat-packed furniture without reading the instructions cannot know where they went wrong unless they go back and read them. That's the same with us and the Bible.

Being able to think, believe, and say what God thinks, believes, and says about you can only be done by reading the Bible and learning from others who teach his Word. It's that simple.

I would not be where I am today if I did not have God's Word to support and teach me. It has been my lifeline without a shadow of a doubt. It is the most precious thing in my world because God used it to undo Satan's lies and to give me hope for my future.

> Your word is a lamp to my feet and a light to my path. (Psalm 119:105 ESV)
>
> Establish my steps and direct them by your word; Let not any iniquity have dominion over me. Deliver me from the oppression of man; so will I keep Your precepts. (Psalm 119:133–134 ESV)

> If you abide in my word, you are truely my disciples, and you will know the truth and the truth will set you free. (John 8:31–32 ESV)

> Faith comes by hearing, and hearing by the word of God. (Romans 10:17 NKJV)

Praise God for all he does for you. This brings you peace as you focus on God's strength and not the problem. When you begin to praise God, you remember that you are not alone in dealing with the situation and that even though you may not see the answer, God is with you and is helping you through.

Arm yourself with heavenly support through constant daily prayer to God and regular support from other Christians. When the enemy attempts to attack, you are then surrounded by other Christians to help you through the battle, as you will for them both practically and through prayer.

Learn to say only what the Bible has to say about you and your future, and obey God's word. It's there for your protection.

CHAPTER 21

Securing Your Territory

Securing your territory is about who you let in
and who you keep out or even kick out.

What I was never taught was that Jesus said confront your brother if they sin against you by speaking the truth in love and involve elders if they will not listen.

> If your brother sins against you, go tell him his fault, between you and him alone. If he listens to you, you have won your brother. But if he does not listen, take one or two bothers along with you, that every charge may be established by the evidence of two or three witnesses. If he refuses to listen to them, tell it to the church. And if he refuses to listen even to the church, let him be to you as a Gentile and a tax collector. (Mathew 18:15–20 ESV)

For some abusers in my life I was able to restore a level of relationship by rebuilding my boundaries, expressing my opinion, standing up to their criticism, and managing their disapproval. But with others, I had to walk away because change was never going to occur and harm was just going to continue toward me.

This was far from easy and something I really struggled with as a Christian and never did lightly but prayerfully.

Abusers will never learn the consequences of their wrong behaviour if we keep condoning it. Then God cannot work in their lives to convict them of their sin and heal them from it.

Abusers still need to be held accountable for their wrong behaviour and face the consequences. Otherwise, our society could never feel safe. That is why we have laws to safeguard against such behaviours and to bring justice.

The Bible teaches us to love one another and forgive those who hurt us. It comes down to the very foundation of the Christian faith. As commanded by Jesus, we are to 'love one another as I have loved you' (John 15:12 ESV), meaning instead of putting ourselves first, we are to put others first. We are to serve, not be served. However, love does not mean you condone abuse, or do not confront abusers, or speak the truth in love.

With forgiveness, it does not automatically mean the relationship will be restored. Forgiveness is the change in your heart and in the attitude you have toward them. It does not mean that they have automatically changed. Therefore, you can forgive someone without being in a relationship with them.

Now when I see signs of abuse, I get out of the relationship quickly when I do not feel safe enough to confront the abuser. I don't owe an explanation to anyone and I certainly don't have to justify myself. I will pray for them and forgive them but I am not there to save them. Jesus came to do that.

A word of caution. As every victim knows it's not as simple as just getting up and walking away. There can be a range of other barriers, depending upon the type of relationship it is, the supports you have access to, accommodation and money you have, and whether there are children or pets involved. Then, of course, there is the potential of how they will react and what they could do.

Remember, abusers will not like you securing your territory. They will retaliate aggressively, either emotionally, physically, or financially. So you must seek help from the beginning to plan your best course of action. Every abusive situation will be different as there are many variables, including whether you are ready to face the reality of having been a victim of abuse.

Sometimes, a wound is too raw to touch, so it needs some time to heal. Talking about certain details of your abuse can just re-traumatise you when you are not ready. Learn to listen to your body and what it is ready for. Never feel obliged to speak about details that you are not ready to, but make sure to seek support.

When you are ready, you can contact a trusted friend, family member, work colleague, teacher, school counsellor, coach, pastor, doctor, clinical psychologist, police officer, or domestic violence service. You can also go to a hospital emergency department to get support; just speak to someone you can trust. If for any reason they do not know what to do, find someone else. Don't stop asking for help until you feel safe in your situation. Remember, you are not expected to have the answers. Just make contact to get support and they can help guide you through.

All of what I have shared is just a glimpse into my experience of abuse. I hope it has begun to unravel some of your questions about abuse so that you can begin to move forward and focus on restoring your future with God.

CHAPTER 22

The Universal Declaration of Human Rights

Knowledge is your power!

WITH ABUSE, BECAUSE YOU ARE TAUGHT THAT YOU HAVE NO rights, it's important to know not just that you have rights, but what they are so you can identify when they are being taken from you. For example, you have the right to speak and you have the right to hold an opinion. Who would have thought! For me, I never knew that I had human rights. I just knew that when you are told to do something by an authority figure, you must obey and you have no right to question them. I encourage you to read The Universal Declaration of Human Rights, adopted in 1948, as it helps to mitigate the lies of an abuser, and remember this.

You have rights.

You have a voice and the right to use it.

You have an opinion and the right to express it.

But, remember,

while you have the right to use your voice to respectfully

express your opinion,

you must also respect the rights of another to use their voice

to express their opinion, respectfully.

This is called having a free will and that's how to show

respect.

Growing in Faith and Hope

CHAPTER 23

How God Works

GOD WORKS BY TEACHING YOU TO SEE LIFE THROUGH HIS EYES. God has taught me a lot through gardening and my animals. He uses things that are relevant to each of us to help us relate to him and understand what he is saying.

When a baby tree is planted, you stabilise it with supports, so when a big storm comes, it doesn't snap. Instead, it uses the strength of the supports as its stability. Meanwhile, it's growing roots (which are its own support system) instead of the ones you provide.

The tree then grows stronger and stronger as it matures and its roots become deeper, so when a storm comes, it can stand on its own. It may have been shaken and lose some branches, but it will not be completely overthrown. This is exactly how God has supported and strengthened me.

Ultimately, the tree can produce fruit and provide shelter for others, and that is what God wants of us. He brings us from a sapling in faith to a maturing tree that can go on to help others to do the same. And this is my hope.

For thirty years, I lived my life as every other human being living the world's way. But then, God literally grabbed me by the scruff of the neck, pulled me back, and said, 'Rosalind, You need to listen to me. You need to take me seriously'. That's when this journey of transformation began thirteen years ago. So, no matter how hard things are, the difference is that today I am not alone in anything I have to face. I always have God with me. He leads, guides, protects, teaches, and disciplines me. He grows me, but above all, he loves me.

I want to share with you that you no longer have to do life alone. God is always by your side if you choose. And, to all the naysayers, I tried your way (the world's way) for thirty years. It killed my sister and it nearly killed me. It was only when I tried things God's way that I was saved from a pit of despair and was able to begin living the life I was meant to live because he set me free.

Like this analogy, imagine a picture showing a little puppet being tenderly created by God and being filled with hope, joy, and a purpose. But then, it is stolen by the devil, tied up with a string, and is now a prisoner. Still, with hope, it tries to play and be happy, but it keeps getting yanked back and controlled. It tries desperately to run away, reaching out in desperation to its ever-fading freedom and God, until finally the devil locks it in its cage forever. Its hope has gone.

Looking out the window of its cell to the beautiful world around, the little puppet cries out for its maker. But, the devil hears and scolds him, and he cowers in fear. God looks for the little puppet, then comes and rescues it. Finding the puppet sitting lifeless, God cuts each string with scissors. The devil's hand is holding the strings not wanting to let go. Gradually, the puppet is set free. Looking bewildered at its hands that are now cut free, it looks up to God.

After putting the devil in jail and tying him up forever, God walks away with the little puppet tucked happily and safely in his arms and nestled in his love, headed for freedom. Finding confidence, the puppet climbs down. Then tenderly and innocently holding the hand of God, the puppet looks on smiling, finally at peace once again, feeling safe and secure.

> God will wipe away every tear from their eyes; there shall be no more death, nor sorrow, nor crying. There shall be no more pain, for the former things have passed away. (Revelation 21:4 ESV)

CHAPTER 24

Know Your Worth and Value

I NEVER UNDERSTOOD THAT MY WORTH AND VALUE ARE IN WHO I am in Christ, not in what I do or have. So what does that actually mean?

When a baby is born to loving parents, they would give their lives to save that child if needed. Even though the child has just put the mother through nine months of pregnancy and excruciating pain during labour, and then keeps the parents up most of the night crying, feeding and being changed, they will drain their own lives to sustain their child's life.

However, in spite of this, the mother and father would give their lives for their baby if they were asked, simply because that baby belongs to them. There is an overwhelming and unexplainable love and protection that can match no other, even before a child is born.

This is how God feels about us, because we are his creation. If you ever wonder what God is like and how to relate to him, remember to think about loving parents, and what they are meant to be like.

They are loving, kind, protective, trustworthy, and faithful. But, they will also discipline to ensure the child is safe, and can grow up independently, and therefore be able to look after itself as an adult.

If for any reason, the child cannot be independent, the parents protect them at all cost and spend their lives caring for them.

The child's worth or value is not in their looks, their talent, their intellect, their ability, or their obedience. The child's worth and value is purely in their parents' love of them. Our worth and value is simply in the fact that, as Christians, we are God's children and nothing can ever change that. He absolutely adores you just because *you are his child.*

If we are disobedient to what God asks us to do by sinning against our conscience or his Word, then he will discipline us as any loving parent would. It is for our own protection to keep us safe. But it doesn't mean that he has stopped loving us or hates us. It just means that he is disciplining our behaviour for our safety and protection.

Think of a child running across the road. Wouldn't you discipline them so they don't do it again and risk being killed by a car? Otherwise, you would be neglectful. The child may be very upset, even crying or angry at you. But what they don't realise is that you are saving their life.

A lot of the time, human beings don't realise that this is what God is ultimately doing: he is trying to save our lives.

Regarding obedience, God made it very clear that I must forgive those who hurt me. I must pray for them and ask God to bless them spiritually, that I must love others the way God loves me, with forgiveness and mercy. And when I have to confront someone, I must do it by speaking the truth in love. He taught me that my bitterness blocks his blessings from coming into my life. And therefore, it will ultimately only hurt me. Now, who doesn't wanted to be blessed?

God also taught me I must have gratitude in my attitude, in doing so it gives him praise. Believe me, these are not easy to do. I failed many times and no doubt will in the future. But when your heart is right before God and you do your best to obey him, he honours you. Now as hard as this sounds, it really works and gets easier the more you practice.

There is a person I know who makes it their mission to show me they hate me. One day, they had a lovely outfit on and God prompted me to tell them they looked nice. In obedience, I did. They gruffly muttered back at me while attempting ignore me as they walked off. Then, no sooner had I walked through the door to where I was going, when another person saw me and came gushing toward me with compliments, relaying what another person had been saying about me.

I was dumbfounded at how good God is and how trustworthy he is to his Word. When you obey him, he gives you strength and victory over the enemy and faithfully rewards you. Love is actually the highest form of spiritual warfare and this is how you pay the devil back for every bit of harm he has ever done to you. 'Love one another as I have loved you' (John 13:34 ESV).

CHAPTER 25

Becoming a Christian

BECOMING A CHRISTIAN IS SIMPLY MAKING A CONSCIOUS choice to turn away from the world's way of living and doing things and choosing to follow God's way of living and doing things. It is choosing to surrender to his Lordship, to his authority, and acknowledging that you need him as the head of your life. It is surrendering everything you are to him by being repentant for your sins, then choosing to turn away from them to follow God. If you want this new life and you want to surrender yourself to God, pray this prayer from your heart.

Prayer of Salvation

Father God I love you. Jesus Christ I believe in you, and that you died for me, you paid for my sin, you took my place, you took my punishment. I'm sorry for the way I have lived, I repent, I turn away from sin and I turn toward you. I receive you into my life today, I ask you to come into my heart to be my Saviour, to be my Lord, to be my God and I give myself to you, take me just the way I am, now make what you want me to be. I believe I'm now saved. I am now a Christian, a Christ follower. I'm on my way to heaven and I want to enjoy the journey, Thank you for loving me, Amen![1]

---

[1] Joyce Meyer, "Joyce Meyer's Salvation Prayer," Accessed from Radio Station Rhema Central Coast 94.9FM. Used with permission of Joyce Meyer Ministries December 31, 2020.

What this means is that you are now part of God's family. Congratulations! If you prayed this sincerely, then you have just been adopted by God and have become his child. Through adoption, you now have the privilege of freely receiving everything God has to give you.

The thing is that when you choose to become God's child and he becomes your Heavenly Father, your enemies had better watch out and batten down the hatches. This is when his Fatherly love really kicks in toward you. He is the Creator of the universe with a Heavenly army, and he will move Heaven and Earth to protect his children.

Just imagine how protective he is of you now that you are his child, considering that he sent Jesus, his only son, to die in your place when you hadn't even chosen him as your Heavenly Father. He loves you that much. So, this is what you have just been adopted into: his unconditional and unending love, his protection, provision, guidance, leading, teaching, mentoring, tenderness, listening, and even his fatherly discipline; his blessings, grace, favour, mercy, forgiveness, justice, vindication, and his victory; his army of warrior angels, guardian angels and messenger angels, his Holy Spirit, and the privilege of calling on his name every moment of every day for his help.

You are no longer alone as you now have God and all of Heaven on your side, and the privilege of God's kingdom, where you will now get to spend eternity.

So, prepare for tests and prepare for trials, but above all, prepare for triumph as you move from fear to faith.

CHAPTER 26

What to Do If I Am the Abuser?

JESUS CHRIST NEVER CAME TO CONDEMN US BUT TO CONVICT us of our sin so that we would repent and turn from our old carnal nature, to become a new creation in him by choosing to be born again and follow him.

We were all born sinners and fall short of the glory of God. But we each get the choice to turn from our sinful nature and follow God or remain as we are.

Jesus taught us to hate sin but love the sinner. My purpose is not to condemn but to help by speaking the truth in love in the hope that it brings healing not only to victims but abusers, too.

However, this is your choice. So, if you do choose, then acknowledge, accept, and take responsibility for your abuse. Pray to God for forgiveness. Lay it all before him in prayer, then ask him to help you and set you free from the sin of abuse. Then give your life to Jesus Christ and follow him by becoming a Christian.

Get professional help and apologise to your victims, only if and when professionally directed. This does not mean returning to the relationship. It is about being accountable and responsible for the wrong choices you made to enable you both to move forward in healing and forgiveness. Then regain trust where it has been broken, remembering it has to be earned; it is not deserved.

Bibliography

Meyer, Joyce. "Joyce Meyer's Salvation Prayer." Accessed from Radio Station Rhema Central Coast 94.9FM. Whom aired a conference, whereby Joyce Meyer spoke the Salvation Prayer which was then written in long hand and used by Rosalind Stewart. Used with permission of Joyce Meyer Ministries December 31, 2020.

Printed in the United States
by Baker & Taylor Publisher Services